# Kick-Start Your Choir

Confidence-boosting strategies

Mike Brewer

FABER MUSIC

# Contents

1. The voice in the classroom   4
2. Starting a choir   6
3. Getting young people to sing   8
4. Sound gestures and conducting   9
5. Programme planning and repertoire   16
6. Preparation and rehearsal   19
7. Basic vocal techniques   23
8. Troubleshooting   29

© 1997 by Mike Brewer
First published in 1997 by Faber Music Ltd
3 Queen Square London WC1N 3AU
Illustrations © 1997 by Harry Venning
Cover design by S & M Tucker
Printed in England by Halstan & Co Ltd
All rights reserved

ISBN 0 571 51749 8

To buy Faber Music publications or to find out about the full range of titles available please contact your local music retailer or Faber Music sales enquiries:
Tel: +44 (0) 171 833 7931   Fax: +44 (0) 171 278 3817
E-mail: sales@fabermusic.co.uk
Website: http://www.fabermusic.co.uk

# Preface

Choral singing is at the heart of music learning in almost every culture. This inexpensive communal activity appears to be thriving globally, helped in several countries by prescribed educational curriculums, encouraging us to find approaches to singing that awaken new interest from young people. Although the outlook is predominantly positive, at the end of the twentieth century, choral singing is challenged by other musical developments. The importance of music technology, evident in the new culture of electronic keyboards and easier access to pre-recorded sounds can, if misused, undermine the unique practice of choral singing.

We have fresh and exciting challenges ahead of us, and it is hoped that the ideas and strategies in this book will be helpful to all involved in choral music whether they are starting, revitalising or improving a choir.

What follows is a compendium of simple, well-tried skills, new perspectives on style and method, and hints on problem-solving which should be of value to anyone working with vocal groups, in the classroom or choir.

I would like to thank those singing teachers and school teachers who, in the course of many a workshop, have helped to shape my thoughts in the preparation of this book. I would also like to thank the staff and members of the National Youth Choir of Great Britain who have been such obliging guinea pigs. Last, but not least, I am indebted to Elspeth Davidson for her contribution to the section *Starting a choir*.

MB

# 1. The voice in the classroom

Traditionally, singing has been seen as one part of a music lesson, and clearly learning and performing a song is an end in itself. What follows in no way detracts from that. There are so many aspects of music which can be appreciated through the voice that it may be worthwhile to spend a moment thinking about the scope which singing offers to the teaching of music.

So here are a few pointers to a more effective use of the voice in the music lesson:

- Start every lesson with a song, preferably on arrival. Choose something well-known or learnt last time. Sing to the class, and let them see that you don't mind using your voice, however insecure you feel. (If worried get some advice from a local singer, or read section 7!)
- Enjoy silence as a framework for all activities. Always start from silence. Use physical ways to achieve this by taking a few seconds to concentrate on posture and breathing (see section 7.1).
- Encourage the use of a range of sounds through vocal games (see 7.1). Invite your singers to listen to themselves and to each other.
- Make connections. When planning a programme of musical activities, think how much could be achieved by using the voice, e.g. include the voice regularly in composition and improvisation. Before playing something on an instrument, sing it first.
- Use the voice in teaching the elements of music: help to develop inner hearing; integrate vocal activity with musicianship; create textures using just voice; construct simple harmony, e.g. sing an arpeggio and invite the children to choose a note from it to hum; play rhythm games using the voice.
- Reinforce the learning of relative pitch, e.g. number the notes of a

scale and play number games such as singing scales by number and making one number silent (1,2,3,–,5) or challenging individuals to sing a specific note by number. Why not teach yourself sol-fa, the most widely used system in the world? (Sol-fa has transformed the learning speed of the new National Youth Training Choir. It really can be absorbed quickly, as the author, a mature student indeed, can testify.)

- When learning something new, de-construct it first. By that I mean identify the musical elements and make games out of them, e.g. take the words of a song and look at the sound production of vowels and consonants (see 7.2). Improvise something – question and answer, sound texture, rhythmic chant. Then look at the structure of the melody and rhythm – spot the repetitions and variations. Improvise on these patterns and especially practise the difficult bits.
- Always aim for a good quality vocal sound, even at the earliest stages of learning.

*Encourage the use of a range of sounds through vocal games*

## 2. Starting a choir

### 2.1 Creating the group

- Any group of people – whether in a school class or not – becomes a choir as soon as it sings together.
- You also have the option of forming a selective choir, using volunteers or picking a team.
- In either case the rewards are numerous:

    for the teacher they can include
    - watching the social group evolve
    - developing musicianship skills through singing
    - helping vocal skills and assurance grow
    - enjoying the activity of performing
    - learning new and progressively challenging music for the group
    - reaping social benefits through cooperation and communal experience
    - gaining responsibility and leadership skills
    - developing musical awareness
    - meeting new people and circumstances through performing

### 2.2 Setting up the operation

- Convince the headteacher of your enthusiasm and of your educational objectives.
- Enthuse your colleagues and don't forget transferable skills, e.g. reading, number, physical, coordination, social and many more.
- Make friends with the PE department, and work harmoniously with them. Get them to help with the physical aspects: breathing,

posture and coordination.
- Involve all the specialists around: nearby singing teachers, artists for posters, linguists for pronunciation, historians and geographers for context, scientists for lighting and sound, pupils themselves (most important) and parents for everything and anything – organising rehearsals, registers, library, discipline (punctuality, having pencils, care of music) tea making, ticket production and sales.

## 2.3 Picking the team

- Involve everyone in singing including the reluctant pupils, instrumentalists who don't see the point and people with learning difficulties (see section 3).
- Convince the football team that the physical act of singing is healthy, strengthens the muscles and the breathing, and will enhance their game.
- Give the boys something special to retain their interest (see 3.)
- Don't mix age groups too widely – they need different approaches and laugh at different jokes.
- Decide whether in your own situation staff involvement will lend support and give out good signals, or if a unified pupil group will be more appropriate.

If you are holding auditions, make them fun, and be sure to include a balance of qualities in the chosen group, e.g. the loud voice which can be taught to blend, the quiet but accurate linchpin who may be able to read music and lead others, the character who will keep the energy going in rehearsal and the soloist with the need to learn to listen to others, etc.

*Involve all the specialists around*

## 3. Getting young people to sing

In purely numerical terms there are in the UK now about three times as many girls' choirs entering competitions at secondary level as mixed and boys' choirs, and most mixed choirs contain very few boys, so what follows has a slant towards the encouragement of boys but may be applied equally to girls.

Here are some strategies:

- Start them young. Make singing a natural activity, at the centre of the school music lesson, whether or not you as the teacher feel confident about your own singing (see section 7).
- Catch them quickly. Day one of school is the time to get everyone singing.
- Find appropriate repertoire. Whatever you choose to do, introduce it within a context, e.g. if most of the group have never sung a hymn, explain its function and use it appropriately.
- Sing enjoyable music. It is good to start with repertoire with which the class is happy and bring them on by making connections with unfamiliar styles through musical elements (similarities of harmony, melody, rhythm or sound).
- Find music from a variety of cultures. In many parts of the world the men take a central singing role in worship, sports and ceremonies. Folk music from around the world is available now in attractive publications.
- Use 'call and response' songs in unexpected situations, e.g. taking the register or asking questions. It really works. Catch them out when they aren't looking.
- Relate the physical act of singing to training for sport. Bring in the PE team you have won over already. Make singing as normal a part of life as eating lunch or catching the bus.

# 4. Sound gestures – towards an understanding of conducting

## 4.1 Gesture and the inspirational upbeat

Before you play a violin you lift the bow. Before you play a wind instrument you expand your breathing apparatus and experience a feeling of lift. The conductor's upbeat achieves all this, and provides the inspiration both of breath and of spirit which leads to making musical sounds. It is the most important part of the choral conductor's art, and controls the framework of silence in which the music is set.

- Every Gesture Betrays Deep Feelings – your choir can sense equally your tension, angularity, insecurity, confidence, involvement, flow, control, understanding of the music.

- Good Balance Demands Flexible Approach – be balanced in your body, mentally alert and responsive to what you hear, so you can create musical sounds in an immediate way.

- Alert Choirs Enjoy Gesture – let the choir feel confidence and pleasure in your sound sculptures. Keep them watching and on their toes.

- FACE them with positive expressions of encouragement.

- Practise preparatory beats, e.g.

    $\frac{4}{4}$ starting on a downbeat – conduct beat 3 (small) 4 (lifting upbeat for breathing in) and 1 (sing).

    $\frac{3}{4}$ starting on third beat – conduct 1 (small) 2 (larger cross beat for breathing in) and 3 (sing). Do the same with other times and bar lengths.

    N.B. with professionals and orchestras the preparatory beat may be omitted; just begin with the upbeat. The same applies in very slow music.

## 4.2 Gesture as image maker

- Your gesture and posture will be mirrored in your choir's response. If you are relaxed, physically balanced and your breathing is deep the choir will subconsciously copy, as they will if you are tense and shallow. This is regardless of your verbal instructions or explanation.
- Your gesture can create the frame within which the choir makes its sounds, and conveys strong emotions through its speeds, degrees of evenness and through subtle changes (see section 4.5).
- Verbal imagery can reinforce gesture. Gesture reaches the right side of the brain, and words the left, so a mixture of the two will enhance understanding in parallel with emotional response. Remember that words convey only about ten per cent of communication, so use gesture much more often than words.
- Your choir will learn to respond to wordless gesture once they have absorbed the meaning you are trying to convey (see section 4.4).

## 4.3 Gesture as support

- Breathing muscles defy gravity, and conducting reinforces the sensation of lifting the air. A sagging beat produces flat and unconnected singing (see section 4.5). Try conducting in $\frac{4}{4}$ with broad horizontal beats (on beat 2 and 3) and notice the singers support the sound better.
- Smooth gestures produce an even flow of air, and thus a *legato* tone.

## 4.4 Gesture as control

- You can't beat time, only keep in rhythm with it. Make sure you can feel the rhythm of your conducting beat as a physical sensation.
- Phrasing derives from breathing. A musical phrase will normally be contained in one sustained breath. Breathe with your conducting.

- Simple techniques of breathing learned by the choir and shown by you in the beat will create an active response (see section 7).
- Economy of gesture will increase effectiveness of response.
- Consistency will increase the choir's security.
- Control should imply care rather than threat.
- Control is positive. Never use negative words.
- Control, paradoxically, releases people's ability to express, rather than confining it.
- Control is only a means to unite the expression of music, not to dominate people. The conductor has a contract with the singers to make cooperative music. If the chemistry is right, then the spirit of the music is released.

## Practical conducting tips

### 4.5 Physical posture and movement

- Stand with a balanced posture. Feel your weight on the balls of your feet. Keep knees flexible and feet apart.
- Keep shoulders down. Imagine you are holding at waist height a large furry animal, quite heavy but gentle. Feel the supporting muscles working – arms, ribs, lower back, stomach, thighs.
- Lift your chosen animal very slightly and feel the concentration of power. Keep elbows slightly out and bring forearms in a little. This creates a good set-up for the choral conductor, which enables your choir to breathe better without directly being asked.
- Practise small movements using upper as well as lower arms. Feel a little upper-arm expansion in the upbeat to assist breathing in.
- For fast tempi use less upper arm than lower, and less wrist movement. Keep your arms fairly close to the body. Imagine you

- are playing a xylophone, with clean bouncing strokes. Remember, the faster the tempo the less the arm movement.
- For slow tempi use lots of flowing arm movement. Use your upper arm freely and make sure the wrist is flexible. Keep plenty of space between arms and body and feel control in your finger tips. Imagine you are conducting underwater.
- Feel control in the fingers. Imagine you are painting a wall 20 metres away with a very long brush, using your conducting hand. Exercise fingertip control. Now try wrist movements, e.g. spreading butter. Try putting your hand on the same side shoulder and conducting with elbows only, gaining control of the upper arm. Now conduct in your 'normal' position, but feel a flexibility in the upper arm, and try using only small, smooth finger movements. Again feel the power in your deep breathing. This works with or without a baton.
- You can conduct *pp* with fingers only. Try it.

### 4.6 Communication, clarity, consistency
- Take the simplest patterns for 2,3, and 4 beats in a bar. See if you can maintain them with the images mentioned before – weight, fluency, no sharp corners, but with laser-clear finger ends.
- Think ahead. Practise beats for starts and stops, changes of tempo.
- Use weight and size of beat for *crescendo* and *diminuendo*. Use large gestures sparingly. They have the same effect as cymbal crashes in the orchestra.
- Practise beating time and shaping phrases together (a challenge when in front of the group, so it needs lots of practice). If in doubt keep movements small and see what response you can get with slight changes in movement. Make it into a game.
- Practise in front of a mirror. Get used to what you will look like to the choir. Keep practising until movements become familiar and subconscious, like when you learned to walk, swim or ride a bike.
- Practise conducting the music you intend to perform, concentrating on speed changes and preparatory beats. Teach your body to

remember the movements so you can relax with increasing confidence in front of the choir.

## 4.7 The interpretative hand

Many conductors use their 'interpretative' hand (usually the left) to mirror the work of the 'conducting' hand. Although this does no harm it is unnecessary; it is far more worthwhile to train it to influence the choir musically. The basic musical uses of your interpretative hand are:

- encouraging good breath support
- cueing entries and cut offs
- interpretation: accents, dynamics, expression, intensity, and mood

*Practise in front of a mirror . . . get used to what you look like to the choir*

Start by keeping your interpretative hand in your pocket while conducting beats and some *crescendo* and *legato* with the conducting hand. Now use the interpretative hand to cut off the sound of the choir at the end of a phrase: use a small lift, like flicking a switch upwards. Lifting at phrase ends will stop the phrase clearly and helps to maintain air flow for the next phrase – hold your furry animal and you'll hold your choir.

Gradual dynamic changes can be achieved by an outward movement of upper arm to encourage breath expansion for *crescendo* and an inward movement (elbows into sides and hands towards you) for *diminuendo*. Lifting your hands for *crescendo* makes the shoulders go up and the choir's breathing becomes shallow; likewise, lowering your hands for *diminuendo* produces dull and airless singing and can lead to flat tuning.

Use the interpretative hand to anticipate new phrases. Look at the singers two beats before, then slightly raise the arm, palm upwards, one beat before, inviting them to join you. On their entry beat, again offer them the sound with a small hand and finger movement – downwards or bouncing up. Now support the conducting hand at important moments with outwardly expanding gestures to give positive images for breath support. This will help produce a rich, rather than a forced tone from singers.

Remember:

- a raised palm invites the choir to sing
- a flat, downward palm invites the choir to stop singing

## 4.8 Intentions

The most important part of communication is having something to say.

If you are uncertain about a piece of music, make yourself answer this list of questions. (You can later modify your performance with the increased awareness gained from the learning process of actually rehearsing.)

- What is the function of the music as a whole?
- What is the mood to be conveyed in the whole piece and in each section?
- Whereabouts in this list of opposites is a particular note or phrase?
  long-short, high-low, quiet-loud, heavy-light, fast-slow, peaceful-aggressive, bright-dark, happy-sad, cold-warm, relaxed-intense, smooth-rough, thin-thick – add your own.
- What colour is the note?
- Is the intensity growing or diminishing?
- What function do the words have? What are they expressing? Which are the important words?

Now see if your intentions are clear yet. Test them on your choir, and consider how well you have communicated them. Absorb your intentions automatically into your performance. Don't do anything without a musical intention in mind.

## 4.9 Gesture and leadership

What you say goes. Allow points to be made by singers, but don't let the flow of your rehearsals be disturbed. Let discussion happen during breaks. Admit your mistakes, and use the experience to improve your preparation next time.

- Be wary of your power, and use it for good.
- Be firm but fair. Win people over by your musical conviction, rather than by words.

*Allow points to be made by singers but don't let the flow of your rehearsals be disturbed*

- Use humour as a positive force, not at someone's expense.
- Never be negative.
- Love the music and thus the musicians.

# 5. Programme planning and repertoire resources

## 5.1 Strategies

- Have a clear view of the function and objectives of your choir. Plan a season of work which sets reasonable programmes in relation to the average ability and level of the singers, the needs of performance and the likely target audience.
- Plan far enough ahead to cover a season of balanced music. Leave enough time to deal with publishers.
- Make regular use of library sets, and persuade your local library to buy in music. Use the nation-wide library loan service. Your local library will give you details.
- Contact music publishers about your needs. Get on useful mailing lists.
- Seek good pieces from colleagues, and share your discoveries with them. Telephone neighbouring conductors.
- Think world-wide. Use the fax machine and the Internet.
- Try something unconventional, even if it scares you a little.

## 5.2 Variety

- Texture – from unison to as many parts as the choir can reasonably handle.
- Style – branch out.
- Sound – vary for different styles (see section 7).
- Expressive techniques – *staccato* and *legato*, dynamics and colours, articulation, phrasing.
- Difficulty – mix challenging music with easier pieces. Sugar the pill. Think of rehearsal time available, and share it between pieces. (see section 6).

- Balance between familiar and new works.
- Stimulation – keep the singers alert with new experiences.

## 5.3 Appropriateness

- Ability and experience of the singers.
- Age of the singers (it's easy to patronise sometimes).
- Range – don't be seduced into repertoire which is uncomfortable for children. However, high notes need not be a problem if singing techniques are developed at a basic level (see section 7).
- Tessitura – be careful about the overall pitch level of a piece. If a great deal of it lies high it will be hard to sustain a good sound, and may cause strain.
- Overall difficulty of performance and learning. Take care over wide leaps in melodies. Children naturally sing stepwise tunes for good physiological and aural reasons; worldwide music reflects this. Pop music retains repetition and simplicity, but more sophisticated musicals may have wide melodic leaps. N.B. some apparently difficult rhythms prove to be aurally memorable, so don't be put off by the appearance of page one.
- Occasion – within worship think of season and function.

    In church or concert hall be aware of acoustics, size of building and expected audience, visibility, general atmosphere, relevance of music to be performed.

    Choose appropriate music for other classes to hear in school, for the foyer of the local theatre, and for the shopping mall.

- Collaborate with the other performing arts. Music for the play, the dance, and the art exhibition can include singing just as well as instruments.

## 5.4 Balance of programme

If you choose a mixed programme, think of:
– a thematic connection or idea
– a consistency of style or mood, or a conscious variety.
You may have a message to put across, or just want to

present people with a stimulating combination of experiences.
- a reasonable length. Better to leave the audience wanting more. Most school concerts are too long. . .
- an entertaining presentation. Don't overdo the verbal introductions, but do relax the audience (and the choir) with a few words.
- Your overall aim is to make the whole experience memorable for performer and audience. Don't be boring in the planning or in the performance.

*Don't overdo the verbal introductions*

# 6. Preparation and rehearsal

## 6.1 Preparation

- Know the score. Learn it gradually over a period of time. Spend lots of 10 minute slots getting to know parts of it. Note especially tempo changes, moments of climax, pauses, and other specific landmarks.
- Be aware of each detail for every voice. Mark in breath points. Try putting final consonants of phrases at the beginning of the next rest. If there's no rest, take a half beat off the last note of the phrase. Be exact. A consonant in time saves pain.
- Spend time on the text. Clarify meaning, and look for the expressive use of sounds.
- Identify points of musical interest and of likely difficulty. Devise strategies for each one, making up games from the component elements – melody, harmony, rhythm, e.g. unusual or new rhythms, leaps in melody, imitation, repetition, use of words.
- Try to hear the whole piece in your head. To assist you, play it on an instrument, or ask someone else to, or listen to any available recordings.

## 6.2 Placing the singers

It generally works well to:
- place the strongest singers towards the middle of their section
- place good sight-singers next to poor ones
- place clear focused voices next to less focused ones
- try different choral formations for different pieces, e.g. men in the middle, or the choir divided into mini SATB groups

### 6.3 Twenty thoughts on rehearsal

- 1. Keep alert in the rehearsal to every sound, listening all the time for blend, balance and intonation, keeping ears and mind open. This is not easy, so try concentrating on just one of those things during a particular practice (see thought 7). Make notes (devise a code to save time) of particular happenings in rehearsal. Look at strategies on your own before meeting the choir again.
- 2. Create precise and reliable times and venues if possible, to avoid potential for misunderstanding and to set patterns. (The author finds this a major difficulty, and offers sympathy!)
- 3. Plan singing sessions to include a mixture of new material, detailed study of previously started pieces and singing right through known music. Start with breathing and energising activities (see section 7). Do the more concentrated work early on. Begin with known material, then relax into systematic work on something new. Then practise shorter sections on a number of pieces. End with a performance of something.
- 4. Start promptly and make maximum use of every minute. If you are standing and doing silent breathing, latecomers will creep in.
- 5. Use 'warm ups' and vocal exercises but make them
    – fun.
    – related to music being learned, e.g. take a few notes and look for repeated patterns, changes, problem intervals or rhythms.
    – positive. The voice really does need to warm up, and games are an ideal way to enhance the development of learning (see section 7).
- 6. Have definite aims, but don't be depressed if you don't get there. Don't ever simply sing through something without a specific intention, even if it is only to see how well the group remembers it.
- 7. Separate the musical elements often in rehearsal. Spend time on words only, rhythm only, melody only, or chording only. The learning speed is increased.

If there are mistakes, look at the problem in isolation rather than singing a whole section again. Troubleshoot, and if helpful make a game out of the problem (see section 8). Assess positive learning. If you have a number of difficult pieces or moments, work at them for less than seven minutes each, and move on. De-construct small difficulties, for example in text or rhythm (those you identified and prepared beforehand, of course!).

- 8. Use the skills of individuals from the outset in helping to teach others. Send people away (trust them) to look at specific short sections. Any room will do, or any corridor. If someone owns a portable instrument, let them take it, or borrow chime bars or recorders. There's always a way.

- 9. Enjoy good tuning from the start. Treat people who are slow to hear pitch with discretion. In the unselected group keep everyone involved. If you have a selected group it may be best to be honest and offer help individually. Improvement can be startling once the person becomes aware. Take the learning process slowly, beginning with simple pitch imitation and then small intervals.

- 10. Cultivate memory. Use silent learning time during rehearsals for, say, 45 seconds. Each member of the choir works at memorising a section alone and without any sound. It works magically. Risk it.

    Try a memory game. Sing aloud and silently alternately according to your hand signal, e.g. holding your hand up could mean sing out loud, and holding it out, palm upwards, could mean sing silently in your head.

    N.B. keep a balance between memorising by ear and sight-singing.

- 11. Be flexible. Alternate periods of concentration with light-hearted moments. (Often the mood dictates itself, but see section 7.3). If a piece is going downhill, introduce variation to maintain interest, e.g. change rhythm, speed, sound (whisper, articulate consonants, or sing vowels only). Stand and sit. Move the choir to new positions for different pieces. (Don't take too long over it!)

Sing in scrambled positions, with each member of the choir placed next to another singing a different part.
- 12. Divide the choir in two. Let them sing to each other in friendly competition.

- 13. Incorporate improvisation regularly. Make up patterns on the theme of your piece. Use chords and clusters, and rhythmic imitation and variation.
- 14. Practise unaccompanied.
- 15. Video rehearsals. Let everyone see who looks alert, has good posture and is watching.
- 16. Sing in foreign languages for the sake of the sounds.
- 17. Listen to what members of the choir say. Form a student committee to organise the details (see section 2.2).
- 18. Know every choir member as an individual. Each has a different starting point in posture, mouth shape, listening, previous experience, ability. If there isn't time in rehearsal, have a separate word with individuals.
- 19. Enjoy sound making. Revel in the variety of textures and colours available with every vowel. Give the group a general or particular objective for the rehearsal. Try inappropriate styles and sounds, to reinforce what you actually want. Let individuals go to the back of the room, listen and comment constructively.
- 20. Always be positive and retain a sense of humour. Try to avoid negative words. Instead of 'you're useless' say 'OK let's try plan B' (see section 4.8).

# 7. Basic vocal techniques

*Our first infant sounds are vocal, uninhibited and physically energised*

Our first infant sounds are vocal, uninhibited and physically energised.

However, we tend to stop using our breath support mechanisms before we start school, and by puberty we are often inhibited socially too. We have to make a positive effort to rediscover a natural and open way of singing.

Each exercise which follows can be made into a fun activity. With younger children it can be associated with a story, an atmosphere or a picture. Get used to experimenting with pure sound. Children love to improvise, not least if the activity can be recorded.

## 7.1 Good use of the body

N.B. some of the following exercises emphasize a particular physical aspect. It is sometimes useful to exaggerate while learning something, and then modify as it becomes absorbed. Do not make a dominating feature of any one aspect. Balance is the key to success.

- Sitting – forward on the edge of your seat, with feet in line with a straight spine, and with weight on toes. Imagine a rope attached to the top of your head, pulling up to the ceiling. Feel tall.
- Standing – feet comfortably apart, muscles seeming to defy gravity, making you feel tall, well-balanced and relaxed. Bend to the left and right, feel the balance. Weight on toes. Lift heels off the ground. Clench everything clenchable, and relax. Stretch arms to the ceiling, feel circulation to the fingers and toes, and feel the ribs rise. (Many stretching and posture exercises can be borrowed from the PE department.)
- Breathing – breathe in naturally, feeling rib expansion, out and up. Take care to keep shoulders relaxed and down. Make up images to reinforce good practice, e.g. imagine you are holding a

shopping bag in each hand, full of groceries. Try holding your breath for a count of 5, then 10. Feel the control and the potential energy.

- Breathe out – with a sigh, then between pursed lips. Hold a finger in front of the lips and blow hard onto it. Feel the concentrated energy. Breathe out in short bursts making 'ss' or 'ff' sounds, like air from a tyre. Try that with hands behind you and fingers on hips. Feel the back muscles in action. Next time you breathe in and out see if you are conscious of the whole lower body giving 'support' in this way. Make up other image games.

- Now feel the lower abdomen expand as you breathe in, and lift the breathing apparatus as you breathe out. Try a long 'ss' and some short 'ft' sounds. Now put your hand on your solar plexus and repeat. Feel whether that area pops forward on the short sounds, e.g. breathe in on a count of 5 and out evenly on a count of 10 using different sounds, 'sh', 'ss', 'ff', and blowing through the lips. Start strongly, then try very quietly, feeling the sensation and the control.

N.B. the diaphragm, hidden inside, cannot move on its own but moves naturally as we manage the airflow, and can be controlled by the muscles we have been using. 'Sing with the diaphragm' is a common cry from teachers. If you feel stomach and back expanding you can be sure that the diaphragm is doing its job.

- Check the inhalation energy. (1.) Breathe in through the mouth. Feel the cold air at the back of the palate. This works well for a quick breath. (2.) Breathe in slowly through the nose. This gives a sensation of warm control and energy, high in the back of the mouth and throat, and is recommended for situations where there is time to do it. N.B. if your first sung note is a vowel, make that shape with your mouth when breathing in. Often when singing a consonant, the following vowel shape can already be there in the mouth, e.g. to sing 'la' make 'ah' shape and flick tongue for 'l'.

## 7.2 Basic soundmaking

- *Open throat.* To avoid a noisy intake of breath, one helpful picture

is to take an imaginary large drink. Feel the throat opening inside.
- *The vocal folds (chords)* vibrate as air passes through. Because they are fragile the control and support of air is important in good and healthy singing. Forcing sounds without controlling the air can be damaging (see section 7.1).
- *Pharyngial resonance.* As the air passes beyond the folds it resonates, as all musical instruments do. In singing the neck is the chief resonator. Make low open sounds to the neutral vowel 'uh' as in 'word', and slide up and down in pitch. Feel the freedom in the back of the neck. Slide higher, gradually changing the sound to 'ah'. Pretend to throw a ball as you reach the top. Hold an imaginary log behind your head and throw it forward as you slide high with the sound. Feel the natural freedom and resonance right up the back of the neck and into the head.
- *Soft palate and resonating passages.* Imagine the sound actually lifts into the head quickly at the start of a note. Call out 'hi' with a very short sound, then with decaying sound (like a rocket descending). Feel the energy and the release. Try 'wow', 'yeow', etc. This enables notes to be reached way above the range normally used in songs. Top notes no longer need be a mountain to climb, but can be felt to be floating in the air.
- *Vowels.* These are the most important aspect of singing because they carry the sound itself, determining its tone colour, intensity, direction and shape. The colour of the sound is refined by jaw, lips and tongue. An open throat enables the air (carrying the sound) to pass cleanly through. The jaw needs to be loosely hanging, not pushed forward and not pressing down. Clenching the teeth, a common fault with young people, creates tension, closes the throat and produces a strangled sound. Don't criticise this, but play games to open the jaw. If one finger can move freely between parted teeth that gives a good approximation of the position for 'ah'.
- *Harmonics.* The vowel colours we hear are formed by the harmonics present in the sound. Moving lip, jaw and tongue positions

alters the proportions of harmonics for each sound and makes vowels change. Lips forward 'oo'. Make gentle cooing sounds to 'oo' feeling the top lip vibrating with focused air, again sliding around in pitch. Feel the resonance in the lips and in front of the teeth. This helps to avoid some versions of 'oo' trapped in the throat. Move lips and tongue through a sequence from 'oo' via 'aw', 'ah' to 'aa' then 'ii' and back again. Sense what the comfortable position is for sounds you like on each vowel. N.B. think always of the sound lifting into the back of the head and forward over the top.

Vowels can be 'opened' and 'closed' with the tongue and lips. Different languages and different regions vary greatly in their vowel sounds (see section 7.3).

Try these: sing 'o' as in 'dog'. Raise the middle of the tongue towards the mid-palate and let the lips go forward. The sound colour darkens and may sound more like 'aw' as in 'paw'. Sing 'i' as in 'pig'. Lift the tongue. Again the sound changes, perhaps to 'ee' as in 'feed'. Try 'ah' as in 'far'. Raise the tongue, and you may sound like 'eh' as in 'fair'. 'e' as in 'egg' with tongue high might sound like a Germanic vowel ('Seele', for example).

Generally open vowels are very good for general blend and pitch retention, and careful use of closed vowels gives great colour and resonance, and helps avoid screeching on high notes.

- Many young singers produce a breathy sound because air escapes at the vocal folds, particularly at the start of a note. However, if the air from below is well controlled the folds can open and close cleanly and the sound starts and stops well, producing a clear round sound. To help achieve this try the following games: make short, quiet sounds like a monkey to 'oo' at varying pitches and in different rhythms. Feel the stomach muscles in control. Now add consonants in front of the vowels, 'moo', 'noo', or 'doo', still feeling the energy in the vowel. In music think of the vowel on the beat and the consonant, however long, before it. This will produce instantly clear rhythm and ensemble, and avoids sluggish starts. To stop the sound cleanly imagine you are cutting it off at the throat, like a switch being turned off. Try it, it works.

- *Resonance through humming.* Hum with lips just touching and teeth apart, then repeat with 'nn' (tongue half-way back) and 'ng' (tongue at soft palate). Feel the air resonate at the back and then 'sympathetically' in the nose. Make up nonsense words, or sing 'ding', 'ring', 'long', etc.

- Concentrating on resonating consonants will vastly develop the overall tone of the choir. Don't forget that 'l' will resonate – and 'zz', 'vv', 'zzh' and 'rr'. *Legato* is created by continuous sound resonating through vowels and consonants. Try singing 'Amen', 'Sanctus', 'never', 'easy', 'ergeben', 'jamais'.

- Plosives will also reinforce the energy, with support from the stomach: 'p' 't' 'k' and then vocalised 'b' 'd' and 'g'. ('k' and 'g' are made by stopping the air through the vocal chords themselves, and will need less energy than the others to sound strong.) An excessive 'attack' sounds unmusical and damages the chords. Try 'pick pocket', keeping the airflow constant through the quick consonants. Flick the tongue and lips while singing a vowel. Try 'Davadava', 'tip o' the tongue', 'red leather yellow leather' – feel the rhythm of the words dance inside you. Make up your own.

- All the activity so far has been aimed at developing the resonance and freedom of high notes, using what is commonly called 'head' voice. Much popular music uses a 'belted' sound from the chest in lower range singing. This is fine provided the breath is supported by the body as described above, but damaging if the sound is pushed straight out from the throat without enough air from below or resonance from above. *Glissando* games from high pitches downwards help retain resonance in the middle range, where the voice is weakest, and down into the chest register. Practise singing downward scales, keeping the 'high' tone.

Most young choral altos are in fact sopranos using the chest voice for low sounds. If the throat is open and the breath is gently supported any singer can produce a full and chorally valuable sound. If you are short of altos add different sopranos for different pieces. Share the load, but note all the above.

To achieve more volume at all registers:
- don't force the sound
- use more air, not more muscle strain
- use more resonance (as described above)

## 7.3 Sound colours and musical styles

The texture of vocal sound and blend can be used in basic ways to create moods and fit different styles of music. In general, open vowels will sound Italian; more closed vowels will sound North European. In rhythmic music from Africa the consonants are often very strong and vowels tend to be closed, whereas in South America strong rhythmic attack goes with open vowels. Children will copy a style or a sound as readily as they will copy an action, and it is sensible to find someone to perform as authentically as possible, on tape if necessary. There is no substitute, however, for copying a live performer (aural, kinetic and visual memory working together).

For many performance styles from the past we can only guess from written material. A very profitable rule of thumb is to remember that in a sense all music derives from the dance. Even the most apparently academic of church compositions reveal a rhythmic drive and a new dimension if treated in this way.

Here are some games:

1. Sing up and down a pentatonic scale with a variety of vowels. Each individual chooses a speed and may hold any note.

2. Choose a rhythmic pattern and let individuals start it at different times.

3. Build up cross rhythms vocally with nonsense sounds.

4. Sing a chord and slide up to the highest note you can sing, then slide down to your original note if you can remember it.

Make up games of your own, and use activities from instrumental music, e.g. question and answer, building up structures, *ostinato*.

# 8. Troubleshooting

**Keeping your choir's engine running smoothly**

*If it ain't broken don't fix it.*

There's a great danger of our giving long-suffering singers lectures on every aspect of the choral art, especially tuning, keeping together and watching. All these can be better achieved through games, e.g. if you have a problem with non-watchers, remember that you need to be worth watching. Be entertaining – unpredictable – positive. Change speeds randomly and catch people out, then enjoy the sensation of positive control of the accelerator and the brake. Steer them through the curves of the phrase. Change gear (conduct differently – with smaller, larger or more angular beats – trial and error is the best way) for hard climbs or rough terrain. Let them enjoy the journey with you.

Don't meddle. Don't try and solve everything in one go. Be like a sheep-dog and look at things from one angle and then another, e.g. if there are problems with rhythm and tuning, work at one for a time and ignore the other. De-construct and reassemble. It's never useful to sing badly, so if the tuning is suffering get the rhythms right without pitch first, then the pitch without rhythm, then put together by degrees, limiting it to just a pair of notes if necessary. Finally have a break or sing something well-known.

## 8.1 To change a flat choir

*Always alter something.*

Physical causes:
- Air pressure – breathing and support. Stand up. Try something from section 7.
- Outlet valve – jaw, lips and tongue (vowels). Adjust and relax any of those.
- Fine tuning – resonators, soft palate. Make some 'pinging' sounds,

and other exercises from section 7.

- Use of gears for high and low notes: open jaw wider when high. Sopranos above E, darken vowels towards 'uh' to remove highest harmonics (screech!). Lips come forward and tongue lifts slightly. Use lots of breath support for low notes, and don't 'push' any notes straight out. Always start and finish with air through the vocal chords, and always feel the air lift, especially at the end of each phrase; your ribs remain out, and the air keeps flowing evenly until the exact millisecond when you stop the note.

Musical causes:

- *Road holding 1.* Direction of phrase. Keep the first note of a phrase in the memory. When the same note comes again test yourself. Is it the same note? You can then remember the notes of a chord. Sol-fa helps beyond measure here too. N.B. listen to the final note right to the end. You need to do two things at once – hear the note you are singing and anticipate the next. Try a game: hold a note on at random, and suddenly move on to the next. See how quickly your singers can respond.

- *Road holding 2.* Harmonic progressions. As chords change be aware of notes in common, and in two-part singing, practise slowly, enjoying each change of interval between the parts, especially where one part stays on the same note and the other moves.

- *Road holding 3.* Scales. They tend to flatten both going up and going down. The main reason (apart from not listening and remembering) is lack of air support. A trick for keeping scales in tune: when ascending press down with elbows wide on an imaginary waist-high bar. When descending hold a heavy (but soft) imaginary animal in wide arms, again waist-high. As you reach the end lift the chosen animal very slightly. Find your own images for supporting the air. (See section 4.5.)

- *Road holding 4.* Psychological causes. Lack of energy, will-power, motivation, tiredness, hunger, boredom. Change something in the singing, e.g. rhythm, speed, key, words, dynamics within the parts, the piece. Tell a joke, take a break.

- *Road holding 5.* External causes. Acoustics of room, stale air, light, temperature, humidity, strong winds, time of day, group mood. Solutions – try another position in the room, another room (if possible), open or close windows, adjust lighting (bring in lights if necessary), bring heater, fan, change time (if possible), otherwise agree to cope, and tell another joke.
- *Road holding 6.* Singers vitally need water. Encourage your choir to bring plastic bottles to the rehearsals.

## 8.2 If with all this energy your choir goes sharp (which it sometimes will) then:

- Relax the shoulders and the jaw, move around a little and regain calm posture, sing gently using controlled breath without force. Slightly darken the vowel sounds by bringing the lips forward, but keep the sound feeling high in the soft palate.
- Stop and do something relaxing for a moment. Practise slow, quiet breathing, e.g. breathe out to a count of 10 using sounds 'ss', 'sh' or 'ff'.

## 8.3 If the choir engine gets out of control it will rush

Keep it in time by tuning into the internal pulse (e.g. if the piece is in crotchets, feel a quaver pulse in your body). If the engine is short of fuel it will slow down. Feed it with energy, adrenalin and good humour, then invite it to watch you.

## 8.4 If the engine splutters or backfires

If voices are not blending or individuals are dominating the sound, hum a phrase of the piece *pp*. Then ask the singers to walk around, and stop them sporadically, making them sing directly to and blend with another member of the choir. Then sing a whole section *pp*. Ask the singers if they can hear their neighbour on each side.

## 8.5 When the rehearsal mood gets really low, or at the end you feel you haven't achieved what you hoped for:

- Remember your choir has an incredibly short memory for music,

and that also applies to moods.
- Tomorrow is another day. A good night's sleep will actually reinforce what has been learnt, and although much will be lost, the learning speed next time will be twice as fast.
- Never tell the choir off. Identify yourself with them as a team, and discuss the next tasks, maybe asking them to look at or think about something specific for next time. Always end with encouragement. Finish the session with a favourite piece, especially one with movement.

## 8.6 Some concluding thoughts

I have had the pleasure of sharing some of the basic points of choral singing with many hundreds of teachers in workshops over the past decade or so. These ideas have all been tried very many times and found helpful to teachers in looking at the basics of the choral art. They do not pretend to be exhaustive, and indeed it is important that in reading these thoughts you apply them as appropriate to your own circumstances, and whatever doesn't work for you, don't use.

Meanwhile I hope very much that the format, the layout and some of the content may meet some of your needs, and that you enjoy sharing some of my musical experiences in this way. There's no substitute for live music making, and anything written gets frozen on the page and may seem more important than intended.

Please don't take any one idea herein and make a 'method' out of it. My own work and ideas evolve week by week and I'm sure yours do too.

Good luck and happy singing!

*Love the music and thus the musicians*